5.

Harriet Tubman

ROBIN S. DOAK

Children's Press®
An Imprint of Scholastic Inc.

Content Consultant
James Marten, PhD
Professor and Chair, History Department
Marquette University
Milwaukee, Wisconsin

Library of Congress Cataloging-in-Publication Data
Doak, Robin S. (Robin Santos), 1963–
  Harriet Tubman / Robin S. Doak.
      pages cm. — (A true book)
  Includes bibliographical references and index.
  ISBN 978-0-531-21595-1 (library binding : alk. paper) — ISBN 978-0-531-21757-3 (pbk. : alk. paper)
  1. Tubman, Harriet, 1820?–1913—Juvenile literature. 2. Slaves—United States—Biography—
Juvenile literature. 3. African American women—Biography—Juvenile literature. 4. African
Americans—Biography—Juvenile literature. 5. Underground Railroad—Juvenile literature. I. Title.
  E444.T82D63 2015
  306.3'62092—dc23 [B]   2014044844

**Front cover: Harriet Tubman leading
the way through a forest**

**Back cover: Tubman statue in Harlem,
a neighborhood in New York, New York**

Find the Truth!

Everything you are about to read is true *except* for one of the sentences on this page.

Which one is **TRUE**?

T or F Harriet Tubman was the first woman to lead a raid for the Union army.

T or F President Abraham Lincoln gave Harriet Tubman a Medal of Honor.

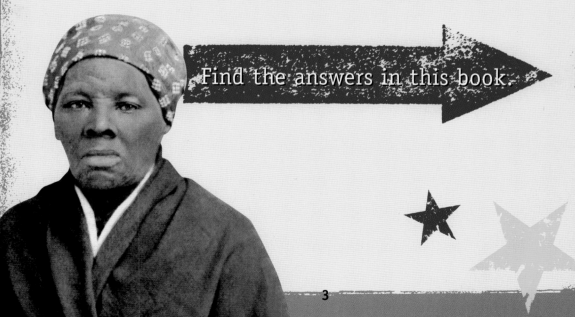

Find the answers in this book.

Contents

THE BIG TRUTH!

Tubman's Friends

William Lloyd Garrison

Tubman (left) poses with family and friends.

A statue of Tubman in New York City was sculpted by artist Alison Saar.

Early Life

Harriet Tubman was born into a world that placed little value on her as a human being. As a black female slave, Tubman faced a lifetime of slavery, violence, and hard labor. But this small, feisty woman with the quick mind and powerful voice would not accept this as her destiny. During her life, she would fight for her and her family's right to live in freedom.

Tubman once said, "There was one of two things I had a right to: liberty or death."

Born a Slave

Harriet Tubman was born Araminta "Minty" Ross, sometime between 1820 and 1822. Her childhood was spent on the eastern shore of Maryland. Minty was born into slavery. Both of her parents were slaves. They were descended from Africans who were kidnapped from their homes by slave traders in the early 1700s. Minty's father was Benjamin "Ben" Ross. He worked on the plantation of his owner, Anthony Thompson. Minty's mother, Harriet "Rit" Green, belonged to a widow named Mary Brodess.

Between 1600 and 1808, nearly 400,000 Africans were enslaved and sent to what would become the United States.

Many slaves on large plantations lived in rows of small, simple cabins or huts.

Rit met Ben when their owners married in 1803. The two slaves married in about 1808. Over the coming years, they would have nine children together.

In about 1810, Mary Brodess Thompson died. Rit and her children became the property of Mary's son from an earlier marriage, Edward Brodess. In 1824, Rit and the children were moved to Brodess's farm several miles away. Ben had to stay on Thompson's plantation.

State law declared that any child born to a slave was automatically a slave.

Hired Out

From a very young age, Minty was expected to work. When she was just five years old, she babysat her younger siblings while her mother worked in Brodess's house.

Later, Brodess hired Minty out to work for other plantation owners. Minty was small, but she became strong. She was put to work doing many kinds of tasks. She set muskrat traps in icy water and worked in the fields. She was also taught to weave.

A cruel master could make life miserable for a slave. One mistress whipped Minty so badly that the beating left scars. When she was a teenager, another master threw a 2-pound (0.9 kilograms) weight at Minty. It hit her in the head and cracked her skull. From that time on, she suffered from **seizures** and headaches. She also experienced narcolepsy, which caused her to fall asleep suddenly and uncontrollably.

A woman beats a slave with a whip.

11

"Next Thing to Hell"

Separated from her family for long periods, Minty grew up lonely and afraid. Hard labor left her weak. She was often sick.

Like other slaves, Minty was not allowed to learn how to read or write. But she was smart, and her mind was active. Although she knew nothing but slavery, she knew that she and her family deserved better. She would later say that slavery was the "next thing to hell."

Like Minty, many slaves dreamed of freedom.

When Minty was young, her master sold three of her sisters.

It was common for enslaved families to be separated.

A New Name

In 1844, Minty married John Tubman, a free black man. Around this time, she also adopted her mother's name, Harriet. Marrying a free man did not make Harriet free. Any children she and John might have would also be slaves.

When Edward Brodess died in 1849, his slaves heard rumors that they would be sold to plantation owners in the South. Slaves in that part of the country often faced even harsher treatment. Harriet decided to escape north to freedom.

Escape was risky and dangerous.

CHAPTER 2

Flight to Freedom

The decision to run away was not an easy one for Harriet. She knew that runaways faced incredible danger on their journey to freedom. Her current owner, Edward Brodess's wife, Eliza, would probably send slave hunters after her. Captured runaways were whipped, branded, and sometimes even killed. Also, Harriet would have to leave family behind in Maryland. Would they be punished after she left?

Harriet's owner offered $100 for her return.

Family members often tried to escape together.

First Flight

In September 1849, 27-year-old Tubman and two of her younger brothers, Ben Jr. and Harry, fled north from Maryland. Harriet had asked John Tubman to come with her. But her free husband did not want to leave Maryland.

Soon after starting out, Ben and Harry became frightened. The journey was hard and long, and they didn't believe they could make it.

After hiding in the woods for three weeks, Ben and Harry decided to turn back. They convinced Harriet to return with them. But she was not ready to give up her dream of freedom. Soon after her return, she ran away again. Her destination was Philadelphia, Pennsylvania, more than 100 miles (160 kilometers) to the north. Although she was alone this time, she would have some important help.

Slaves faced exhaustion and hunger when they escaped.

17

Before she set out, Tubman had told her plans to a friendly white woman. Some historians think this woman was a Quaker. Quakers are members of a religious group that opposed slavery. The woman gave Tubman a piece of paper with two names on it. They were the names of people who would help Tubman hide during her escape. She also told Tubman how to get to the home of the first person.

Many white and free black people worked to end slavery and help slaves escape.

The peak years of operation for the Underground Railroad were from 1830 to 1865.

The people who helped Tubman were part of a secret organization called the **Underground Railroad**. The group included Quakers, **abolitionists**, free African Americans, and others. People called conductors hid runaways during the day and led them to the next "station," or safe place, at night.

Conductors and escaping slaves used the North Star as a guide. The North Star is a bright star that remains fixed in the same place at night.

Tubman did not stay in Philadelphia long before she decided to go back south.

Tubman arrived safely in Philadelphia, probably in late 1849. Little is known about her exact route. It was important to keep this kind of information secret so future runaways would not be caught.

In Philadelphia, Tubman found a place to live. She worked as a maid at a hotel and made new friends. But Tubman missed her loved ones and worried about them. She decided to return to Maryland and guide her family to freedom.

The Fugitive Slave Act

In 1850, Congress passed the Fugitive Slave Act. The law required officials in free states to cooperate with slave owners. This made it easier for owners to find and capture slaves who had escaped to the North. Runaways who had lived in freedom for years now had to worry about being turned over to slave hunters. As a result of the cruel law, many black people in the Northeast fled to Canada.

CHAPTER 3

Becoming Moses

Beginning in 1850, Harriet Tubman risked her life over and over to rescue her loved ones from slavery. Disguising herself as an elderly man or woman, she sneaked back into Maryland 12 or 13 times. Her bravery and determination made her the most famous conductor on the Underground Railroad. Over about 10 years, Tubman personally guided about 70 people to safety. She indirectly helped dozens more by aiding their escape, though she did not lead them herself.

In 1851, Tubman learned her husband had remarried.

The Route to Freedom

Tubman first returned to Maryland in December 1850. She rescued her niece Kessiah and Kessiah's two children. In later trips, Tubman rescued her four brothers, three of them in a single trip in 1854. In 1857, she rescued her parents.

Tubman escorted people along a 650-mile (1,046 km) route through Pennsylvania and into New York. Then they crossed a bridge over the Niagara River into Canada and safety. Slave hunters could not pursue runaways in Canada.

Bad weather could make a runaway slave's journey north very difficult.

Tubman was very religious. She said God gave her visions of the future.

From the Canadian border, Tubman and her group traveled more than 10 miles (16.1 km) to St. Catharines, Ontario. For many trips, Tubman made this her home base. Many of the escaped slaves settled there.

Before long, Tubman's trips became well known among abolitionists. She was nicknamed Moses, after the figure in the Bible who freed his people from slavery.

Tubman was a successful conductor. She once said, "I never ran my train off the track and I never lost a passenger." The keys to Tubman's success were her bravery, determination, and intelligence. She used many different methods to get runaways out of Maryland. These ranged from horses and wagons to boats and even real trains. She used her own money to bribe reluctant helpers and officials.

Timeline of Tubman's Trips on the Underground Railroad

About December 1849

Tubman escapes to Pennsylvania with the help of Underground Railroad conductors.

December 1850

Tubman makes her first trip back to Maryland and rescues her niece and others.

Tubman sang songs to communicate when there was danger and when it was safe. She also carried a pistol with her on her trips. She was ready to use it to avoid being captured—or to convince a frightened runaway to keep going. On one trip, Tubman even used a **sedative** to quiet a crying baby and save the group from capture.

Christmas 1854

Tubman rescues three of her brothers: Robert, Henry, and Ben Jr.

May 1857

Tubman goes back into slave territory to guide her parents out of Maryland.

December 1860

Tubman makes her last trip as a conductor, rescuing several adults and a baby.

Tubman gave speeches to share her story and gather people's support to end slavery.

People in Auburn, New York, knew Tubman as "Aunt Harriet."

Making a New Life

In 1859, Tubman settled in Auburn, New York. There, she bought a small wood-frame home. She and her parents settled into a life of freedom.

Tubman made her last journey along the Underground Railroad in 1860. However, she did not slow down. She spoke at abolition meetings, church services, and other gatherings. Although unable to read or write, Tubman spoke beautifully and powerfully. Her speeches moved many people to action.

Saving Charles

One of Tubman's most daring rescues took place while she lived in Auburn. In 1860, escaped slave Charles Nalle was captured in nearby Troy. Tubman happened to be visiting Troy at the time and decided to help. When officials had Nalle outside, Tubman grabbed him. She, Nalle, and other local abolitionists tried to run, but did not get far before Nalle was recaptured. Not giving up, the rescuers broke into the building where he was held and freed him.

Tubman and Charles Nalle try to run from the courthouse in Troy, New York.

Tubman's Friends

Through Tubman's efforts, she met many other people who were important in the abolition movement.

Frederick Douglass

Like Tubman, Douglass was an escaped slave from Maryland's eastern shore. He was also a well-known abolitionist. Tubman may have used Douglass's home when helping runaways flee to Canada.

John Brown

Tubman met with Brown and supported his plan to start an armed rebellion to end slavery. Brown admired Tubman's bravery and nicknamed her the General.

Susan B. Anthony

Anthony was an outspoken supporter of women's rights. She also argued for the end of slavery. She and others later involved Tubman in the fight to give women the vote.

William Lloyd Garrison

This famous writer and abolitionist was the first to call Tubman "Moses." He published an antislavery newspaper called *The Liberator*.

Lucretia Coffin Mott

A Quaker and abolitionist, Mott helped Tubman hide runaway slaves. She convinced Tubman to settle in Auburn, New York.

Union soldiers battle during the Civil War.

Fighting for Freedom

In the early 1860s, the national debate over slavery came to a head. In April 1861, war broke out in the United States between the Northern free states and Southern slave states. Tubman quickly took action. Throughout the war, she did everything she could to support the North, or the Union.

Tubman earned money during the war by selling pies, gingerbread, and root beer.

Taking Action

With the start of the Civil War, Tubman saw the chance to help free all slaves. If the Union won, it could force the abolition of slavery throughout the South. In early 1862, Tubman sailed to South Carolina and offered her services to the Union army. She worked as a cook and an army nurse. She tended wounded and sick black soldiers as well as newly freed slaves. Often, she used her own remedies and medicines.

Doctors and nurses were in high demand during the Civil War because of the vast number of wounded soldiers.

For more than 30 years, Congress refused to pay Tubman any retirement money for her Civil War services.

Tubman also found jobs for the hundreds of slaves escaping to the Union army for safety. With money from the government, she set up a "washhouse" in South Carolina. There, former slaves could wash and sew clothes for Union soldiers.

Carrying a rifle, Tubman also scouted and spied for the Union. She recruited other former slaves to help her. Together, they risked death to discover and report on the locations of Southern troops.

The Combahee River Raid

In June 1863, Tubman got right into the thick of the action. She led scouts up the Combahee River in South Carolina. She reported back to Union colonel James Montgomery on the number of **Confederate** troops in the area. She also told him the location of underwater **mines** in the river. With this information, Montgomery and Tubman planned a raid of the area. Tubman was the first woman to plan and lead an armed raid for the Union.

The small raiding party sailed three gunboats up the river. They attacked plantations along the shore, taking Confederate supplies and setting some plantations on fire. Thanks to Tubman's information, they avoided the river's mines.

The gunboats blew whistles to call to nearby slaves. Hearing them, slaves of all ages fled to the river. They tried to crowd onto the ships, desperate to escape. To keep them calm, Tubman sang. The raid freed more than 700 slaves.

Tubman and her fellow spies used information they had gathered to safely navigate the Combahee River.

38

Later Years

The Civil War ended in April 1865. The North had won, and slavery in the United States ended forever. Tubman returned to her home in Auburn, New York. However, her last years were overshadowed by **poverty**. She worried about making enough money to care for her aging parents. Tubman herself was also growing older, and her health was beginning to fail. Yet Tubman continued to fight for causes she believed in.

In 1865, Tubman was injured when a conductor forced her off a train.

A National Celebrity

Tubman devoted the rest of her life to supporting the many family members who lived with her. She set up a small brick-making business in her backyard. In 1869, a biography about Tubman increased her fame. Sales of the book helped her repay some of her debts.

In the 1880s and 1890s, Tubman began traveling again. This time, she spoke for women's rights. She joined the National Woman **Suffrage** Association.

Tubman opened the Harriet Tubman Home for the Aged and Infirm (below) near her home in Auburn.

Nelson Davis

Born into slavery in North Carolina, Nelson Davis escaped the South before the Civil War. During the war, he fought on the side of the Union. Davis met Tubman in 1866 when he boarded at her home. The pair fell in love, married, and adopted a daughter named Gertie. They remained together until Davis's death from **tuberculosis** in 1888.

Tubman (left) with her daughter, Gertie, (center) and husband, Nelson Davis

People from across the United States attended Tubman's funeral.

Queen Victoria of the United Kingdom sent Tubman a silver medal and invited her to visit.

Final Years

On March 10, 1913, after a lifetime of action, 91-year-old Harriet Tubman died of **pneumonia**. She died at the Harriet Tubman Home for the Aged and Infirm. This was a charity home that she had purchased and helped found. At her funeral, hundreds of people turned out to pay their last respects to the Moses of her people.

Legacy

More than 100 years after her death, Tubman is still honored for her bravery, determination, and kindness. She serves as an example to those fighting for freedom around the world. Today, schools across the United States are named for her. Statues and plaques remind us of her deeds. Historians continue to study her, trying to learn as much as possible about this brave American. Tubman's lessons are as timely today as they ever were. ★

This statue of Tubman in New York City is just one of many memorials celebrating Tubman's life.

Year Tubman was born: Sometime between 1820 and 1822

Place Tubman was born: Dorchester County, Maryland

Date Tubman most likely first reached freedom: December 1849

Places Tubman lived: Dorchester County, Maryland; Philadelphia, Pennsylvania; St. Catharines, Ontario, Canada; Auburn, New York

Number of times Tubman traveled to Maryland to rescue slaves: 12 or 13

Number of people Tubman led out of slavery: About 70

Day Tubman died: March 10, 1913

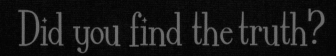

Did you find the truth?

T Harriet Tubman was the first woman to lead a raid for the Union army.

F President Abraham Lincoln gave Harriet Tubman a Medal of Honor.

Resources

Books

Cline-Ransome, Lesa. *Words Set Me Free: The Story of Young Frederick Douglass*. New York: Simon & Schuster Books for Young Readers, 2012.

Norwich, Grace. *I Am Harriet Tubman*. New York: Scholastic, 2013.

Osborne, Mary Pope, and Natalie Pope Boyce. *Heroes for All Times*. New York: Random House, 2014.

Visit this Scholastic Web site for more information on Harriet Tubman:

★ www.factsfornow.scholastic.com
Enter the keywords **Harriet Tubman**

Important Words

abolitionists (ab-uh-LISH-uh-nists) — people who worked to end slavery permanently

Confederate (kuhn-FED-ur-it) — having to do with the Confederacy, or South, before and during the Civil War

mines (MINEZ) — bombs placed underground or underwater

pneumonia (noo-MOHN-yuh) — a serious disease that causes the lungs to become inflamed and filled with a thick fluid that makes breathing difficult

poverty (PAH-vur-tee) — the state of being poor

sedative (SED-uh-tiv) — a drug that makes a person calm or sleepy

seizures (SEE-zhurz) — sudden attacks of illness caused by abnormal brain activity

suffrage (SUHF-rig) — the right to vote

tuberculosis (too-bur-kyuh-LOH-sis) — a highly contagious disease caused by bacteria that usually affects the lungs

Underground Railroad (UHN-dur-ground RAYL-rode) — a network of people and places that helped slaves from the South escape in secret to free states in the North or to Canada before the Civil War

Index

Page numbers in **bold** indicate illustrations.

About the Author

Robin S. Doak has been writing for children for nearly 25 years. A graduate of the University of Connecticut, Robin loves writing about history makers from the past and the present. She lives in Maine with her family.